EYEWITNESS TO HISTORY

FREDERICK DOUGLASS

in his own words

Gareth Stevens
Publishing

By Nicole Shea

Please visit our website, www.garethstevens.com. For a free color catalog of all our high-quality books, call toll free 1-800-542-2595 or fax 1-877-542-2596.

Library of Congress Cataloging-in-Publication Data

Shea, Nicole.
Frederick Douglass in his own words / by Nicole Shea.
    p. cm. — (Eyewitness to history)
Includes index.
ISBN 978-1-4824-3288-6 (pbk.)
ISBN 978-1-4824-3289-3 (6-pack)
ISBN 978-1-4339-9898-0 (library binding)
1. Douglass, Frederick, — 1818-1895 — Juvenile literature. 2. Abolitionists — United States — Biography — Juvenile literature. 3. African American abolitionists — Biography — Juvenile literature. I. Shea, Nicole, 1976-. II. Title.
E449.D75 S44 2014
973.8—dc23

First Edition

Published in 2014 by
Gareth Stevens Publishing
111 East 14th Street, Suite 349
New York, NY 10003

Copyright © 2014 Gareth Stevens Publishing

Designer: Katelyn E. Reynolds
Editor: Therese Shea

Photo credits: Cover, p. 1 (Frederick) Hulton Archive/Getty Images; cover, p. 1 (background illustration) Stock Montage/Getty Images; cover, p. 1 (logo quill icon) Seamartini Graphics Media/Shutterstock.com; cover, p. 1 (logo stamp) YasnaTen/Shutterstock.com; cover, p. 1 (color grunge frame) DmitryPrudnichenko/Shutterstock.com; cover, pp. 1–32 (paper background) Nella/Shutterstock.com; cover, pp. 1–32 (decorative elements) Ozerina Anna/Shutterstock.com; pp. 1–32 (wood texture) Reinhold Leitner/Shutterstock.com; pp. 1–32 (open book background) Elena Schweitzer/Shutterstock.com; pp. 1–32 (bookmark) Robert Adrian Hillman/Shutterstock.com; pp. 4, 5, 14, 20–21 Hulton Archive/Getty Images; p. 7 USHistoryImages.com; pp. 9, 11, 23 Library of Congress; p. 10 Chicago History Museum/UIG/Getty Images; pp. 13, 19, 24–25 (photo) Fotosearch/Getty Images; p. 15 Stock Montage/Getty Images; p. 16 Scewing/Wikipedia.com; p. 17 Quadell/Wikipedia.com; p. 24 (poster) Archive Photos/Getty Images; p. 27 National Park Service: Frederick Douglass National Historic Site/Wikipedia.com.

Printed in the United States of America

CPSIA compliance information: Batch #CW14GS: For further information contact Gareth Stevens, New York, New York at 1-800-542-2595.

CONTENTS

Frederick Douglass's Early Life 4

Learning to Read 6

Escape! 8

New Life, Old Problems 12

Speaking Out Against Slavery 14

Autobiography 16

In Europe 18

Return to the United States 20

The Civil War 22

Life After the Civil War 26

The Passing of an American Legend 28

Glossary 30

For More Information 31

Index 32

*Words in the glossary appear in **bold** type the first time they are used in the text.*

FREDERICK DOUGLASS'S *Early Life*

MORE TO KNOW

During his lifetime, Douglass wrote three **autobiographies**.

In February 1817 or 1818, Frederick Douglass was born a slave with a different name: Frederick Augustus Washington Bailey. At that time in the United States, over 1 million black people were held as slaves. Because slaves weren't considered important enough to keep records for, Frederick didn't know much about his early life, including his birth date. He chose February 14 as his birthday.

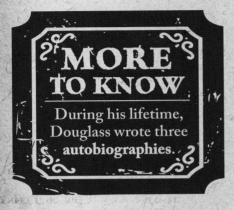

Slave children had a life of hardship ahead of them. They were often sold at a young age.

Frederick Douglass, about 1855

During Frederick Douglass's early life, the practice of slavery was slowly disappearing around the globe. In England, the government had declared the buying and selling of slaves illegal in 1807. It became against the law to own slaves there in 1834. But the United States still held on to the practice, particularly in the South where plantations used slaves in the fields. In the North, factories and businesses used **immigrant** labor and had little need for slaves.

In his autobiography, *Narrative of the Life of Frederick Douglass, an American Slave,* he wrote: *"I have no accurate knowledge of my age, never having seen any* **authentic** *record containing it."* He also knew very little about his mother or father. He only saw his mother a few times at night, and his father may have been his owner, Aaron Anthony. Frederick was separated from his mother when he was still very young.

LEARNING
to Read

A NEED TO READ

Many Southern states had laws forbidding the teaching of slaves to read and write. Owners could be fined or imprisoned. Yet, some did teach their slaves so they could keep records and do other tasks. This made them more valuable. Whether slaves were forbidden to or not, they often shared their knowledge with other slaves. Some, like Frederick Douglass, used their skills to write stories of their captivity called slave narratives.

When Frederick was only 8 years old, he was sent to Baltimore, Maryland, to be a servant to a man named Hugh Auld. Although it was against state law, Auld's wife, Sophia, taught Frederick the alphabet. Her husband stopped this as soon as he found out, saying: *"If you teach him how to read, he'll want to know how to write, and this accomplished, he'll be running away with himself."* He meant Frederick would want to escape a life of slavery if he learned to read. Frederick remembered this as the *"first . . . anti-slavery lecture"* he had ever heard and quickly decided to continue learning.

This was an important moment in the young boy's life. He continued to learn to read from the other children in the neighborhood.

Sophia Auld taught Frederick the alphabet and some small words, too. He later said, "Once you learn to read, you will forever be free."

MORE TO KNOW

Frederick Douglass was such a good student he even organized a school to teach other slaves how to read.

ESCAPE!

In a way, Hugh Auld was right. Frederick became unhappy with his life as a slave. *"I often found myself regretting my own existence, and wishing myself dead,"* he wrote. But he kept alive the *"hope of being free."* He read about the abolition of slavery in newspapers and dreamed of his freedom. He decided to teach himself to write to help him flee. He tried but failed to escape in 1833 and 1836.

MORE TO KNOW

Because Anna Murray's parents had been freed by their owner just a month before she was born, she was free.

Then, in 1837, when Frederick was working on the docks of Baltimore, he met a free black woman named Anna Murray. She worked as a servant for a wealthy Baltimore family. Together, they came up with a plan for his escape to New York City. Anna sold her bed to buy a train ticket for Frederick.

Frederick might never have escaped without the help of his future wife, Anna Murray. →

8

THE UNDERGROUND RAILROAD

Many escaping slaves were helped by a secret society and collection of routes called the Underground Railroad. People called "conductors" guided escaping slaves, or "passengers." The houses where they hid were called "stations," and the owners of the houses were "station masters." They had secret passages to help slaves reach the northern free states or even Canada, where slavery was against the law and the slaves could finally be free.

To help him in his escape, Frederick disguised himself as a sailor. Anna Murray gave him clothes that sailors often wore during that time: a red shirt, a sailor's hat, and a scarf around his neck. Luckily, thanks to his work in the shipyard, he could blend in: *"My knowledge of ships and sailor's talk came much to my assistance, for I knew a ship from stem to stern . . . and could talk sailor like an 'old salt.'"*

SO CLOSE

Frederick Douglass's experience escaping shows how divided the United States was about slavery. Just a few miles or a body of water could separate freedom and slavery. For a slave, life as a free person often seemed so close. Douglass wrote of planning his escape from Baltimore: *"Only think of it; one hundred miles straight north, and I am free! Try it? Yes! God helping me, I will. It cannot be that I shall live and die a slave."*

This is an artist's idea of Frederick Douglass's escape to freedom.

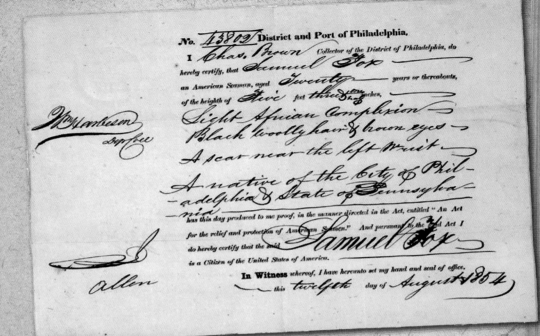

Seaman's Protection Certificate

To complete his disguise, he borrowed an official paper from a friend called a "Seaman's Protection Certificate" to prove that he was a free man and a sailor. Although the paper described his friend and not him, the train conductor believed Frederick and let him continue on to Philadelphia.

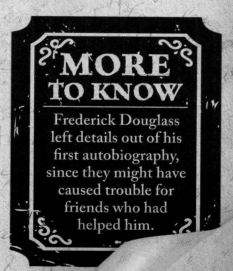

MORE TO KNOW

Frederick Douglass left details out of his first autobiography, since they might have caused trouble for friends who had helped him.

NEW LIFE,
Old Problems

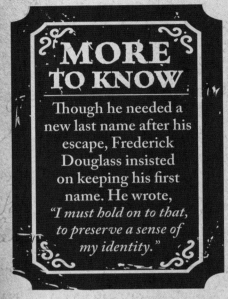

MORE TO KNOW

Though he needed a new last name after his escape, Frederick Douglass insisted on keeping his first name. He wrote, *"I must hold on to that, to preserve a sense of my identity."*

Once Frederick was safe in New York, he sent for Anna. They were married by a minister who was also an escaped slave. At first, Anna and Frederick used the last name of "Johnson," since Frederick couldn't use the name "Bailey" for fear of capture. But Frederick eventually chose the last name of "Douglass." Anna and Frederick Douglass settled in New Bedford, Massachusetts.

Even though Douglass was a free man, he still faced many difficulties in the North. Once, when he tried to get a job as a shipyard **caulker**, the white workers threatened to quit if he was hired. This showed him there was still a long way to go for equality. He wrote, *"People might not get all they work for in this world, but they must certainly work for all they get."*

One of the challenges escaped slaves faced was how to find work to start a new life. Many found that they weren't welcomed in the North. Ex-slaves sometimes offered to work for little money, so white workers who wanted more money had fewer job opportunities. Escaped slaves and free blacks often lived in the same neighborhoods. They did this to avoid capture by slave owners and because some white neighborhoods weren't accepting of them.

Frederick and Anna had five children: Rosetta, Lewis, Frederick, Charles, and Annie.

13

SPEAKING OUT
Against Slavery

ABOLITION

People had been working against slavery since its introduction to the American colonies in the 1600s. There were many reasons. For some, slavery was against their religious beliefs. Others believed it was against the rights of all humans, and still others knew it was just wrong. But while many didn't actively support slavery, they didn't fight it. They didn't want to give up the riches the practice had brought to them.

As an escaped slave, Frederick Douglass became interested in the abolition movement. He attended speeches given by William Lloyd Garrison, the famous antislavery speaker. In 1841, when at an antislavery **convention** in Nantucket, Massachusetts, Douglass was invited up to the stage to give a speech. Although he was nervous and embarrassed, he told a powerful story of his life as a slave.

William Lloyd Garrison

Garrison was so impressed that he invited Douglass to be a speaker for the Massachusetts Anti-Slavery Society. Douglass *"was **reluctant** . . . I had not been quite three years from slavery and was honestly distrustful of my ability."* However, *"the cause was good,"* and so Douglass finally agreed. But audiences weren't always ready to listen. Some mocked him. Sometimes, he was even attacked.

MORE TO KNOW

Douglass's friends in the Massachusetts Anti-Slavery Society told him it was better if he didn't sound too educated when he spoke because people wouldn't believe he had been a slave. But Douglass wanted to be himself.

Once, an angry mob chased Douglass until he was rescued by a friendly **Quaker** family. He broke his hand during this close escape. It never healed properly.

15

AUTOBIOGRAPHY

In 1845, Douglass published his first and most famous work, *Narrative of the Life of Frederick Douglass, an American Slave.* He said he wrote it *"sincerely and earnestly hoping that this little book may do something toward throwing light on the American slave system, and hastening the glad day of deliverance to the millions of my brethren in bonds."* It was a best seller in the United States and in Europe.

MORE TO KNOW

Within 3 years, Frederick Douglass's book was reprinted nine times, with over 11,000 copies. It was also translated into French and Dutch.

However, the book also caused problems for Douglass. In it, he had told everyone he was an escaped slave. According to the laws of the time, if his owner could catch him, he could force Douglass to go back to Maryland. Douglass had to leave the country.

Frederick's actual signature:

Frederick Douglass

NARRATIVE

OF THE

LIFE

OF

FREDERICK DOUGLASS,

AN

AMERICAN SLAVE.

WRITTEN BY HIMSELF.

BOSTON:
PUBLISHED AT THE ANTI-SLAVERY OFFICE,
No. 25 CORNHILL
1845.

SPREADING IDEAS

During Frederick Douglass's time, there was no television, Internet, or radio. Many of the most important ideas of the day were passed through speeches and in newspapers that printed people's speeches. Men and women who could speak well, such as William Lloyd Garrison and Frederick Douglass, became so famous that crowds would form to hear them speak, even if they disagreed with the speakers' ideas.

Because it was so well written, some people thought that Douglass's book couldn't have been written by an escaped slave.

In EUROPE

On August 16, 1845, Douglass set sail for Europe, a trip that would be an eye-opening experience for him. In wonder, he wrote in a letter about his time in Ireland: *"I am seated beside white people—I reach the hotel—I enter the same door—I am shown into the same parlour—I dine at the same table—and no one is offended.... I find myself regarded and treated at every turn with the kindness and **deference** paid to white people."* He found he was given the same respect as anybody.

Similarly, when he was in England later, Douglass said that he was treated not *"as a color, but as a man."* Douglass spent 2 years in Europe giving speeches, and he gained many friends for the abolition movement back in the United States.

A KINDRED SPIRIT

Many Irish, in particular, welcomed Douglass because they saw him as someone who knew what **oppression** was. Although they weren't slaves, many Irish wanted freedom from England, the governing country that for years had prevented them from owning property, attending colleges, or holding office. Oppression wasn't always about slavery; it was often about denying others rights through unfair laws. The way Douglass spoke out against injustice inspired many people outside of the United States.

During his travels, Douglass met many important people, including the famous Irish leader Daniel O'Connell, who opposed slavery so much that he refused to shake hands with a slaveholder.

MORE TO KNOW

Douglass was able to return safely to the United States when two British women, Ellen and Anna Richardson, purchased his freedom. At age 28, Douglass became a free man.

RETURN
to the United States

When Douglass returned to the United States, he started a newspaper called the *North Star*. Through his writing, he fought for the rights of all people, not just slaves. He supported the fight for women to gain the right to vote.

Abolitionists and **suffragists** sometimes disagreed. Though almost all suffragists supported abolition, some abolitionists thought that the fight for women's rights should wait until slavery was ended. Others thought women shouldn't be able to vote at all. Douglass, however, said that not giving women the right to vote

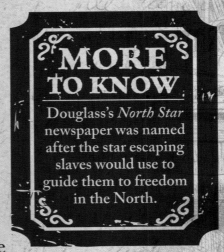

MORE TO KNOW

Douglass's *North Star* newspaper was named after the star escaping slaves would use to guide them to freedom in the North.

Douglass became the first African American nominated to be the vice president of the United States by the prosuffrage Equal Rights Party in 1872.

was hurtful to *"one-half of the moral and intellectual power of the government of the world."* He was present at the first convention for women's suffrage at Seneca Falls, New York, in 1848.

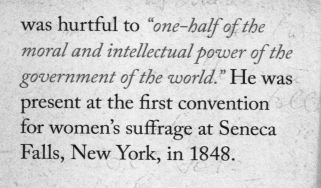

NOT ALWAYS ALLIES

In many ways, women's suffrage and abolition should have been linked, since both were trying to fight for the rights of large portions of the population. However, many believed linking their causes could cause problems. Some people thought if women's suffrage and the abolition of slavery were pushed too hard at once, neither would be achieved since too much change at once could scare voters. These people chose to push for either suffrage or abolition first.

The CIVIL WAR

WHAT ARE WE FIGHTING FOR?

Like many wars, the American Civil War had several causes. For the South, leaving the Union was about the rights of states against the national, or federal, government, including the right to slavery. For many in the North, it was about preserving the nation. For abolitionists, it was about ending slavery. As a result, families often disagreed about the war, pitting brother against brother and child against parent. Some brothers even fought on opposite sides.

When the American Civil War broke out in 1861, President Abraham Lincoln stated that the war's aim was to keep the nation together. But in 1863, Lincoln enacted the **Emancipation** Proclamation, which freed the slaves in the rebelling states. Frederick Douglass became an occasional advisor to Lincoln.

In *Life and Times of Frederick Douglass*, Douglass said he told the president he would *"go into the rebel states, beyond the lines of our armies, and carry the news of emancipation, and urge the slaves to come within our boundaries."* Douglass and Lincoln knew that if peace came too soon, it might

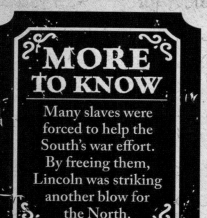

MORE TO KNOW

Many slaves were forced to help the South's war effort. By freeing them, Lincoln was striking another blow for the North.

"leave still in slavery all who had not come within our lines." Frederick Douglass also persuaded Lincoln to let black Americans fight in the North's Union army against the South's Confederate forces.

Douglass (right) later wrote that Lincoln (left) was "the black man's President: the first to show any respect to their rights as men." He was sometimes critical of the president's actions, however.

Frederick Douglass played a big part in signing up blacks for the Union army. He thought fighting for the Union was a way for blacks to become American citizens: *"Once let the black man get upon his person the brass letters U.S., let him get an eagle on his button, and a musket on his shoulder and bullets in his pockets, and there is no power on*

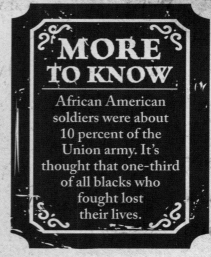

MORE TO KNOW

African American soldiers were about 10 percent of the Union army. It's thought that one-third of all blacks who fought lost their lives.

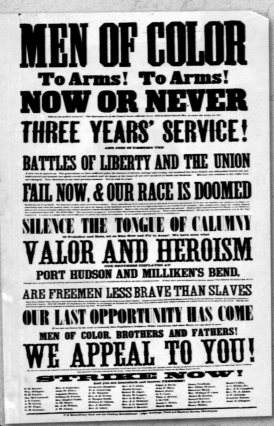

← Civil War recruitment poster

earth which can deny that he has earned the right of citizenship in the United States." Douglass even personally signed up two of his sons, Charles and Lewis, to join a *"gallant and strong"* unit.

However, among other unfair practices, black soldiers weren't paid as much as white troops. Douglass worked to convince Lincoln to change this policy.

Congress passed a bill making pay for black and white soldiers equal in 1864.

EVEN MORE DANGER

The Confederates threatened black Union soldiers wouldn't be treated as regular prisoners of war if caught. They said they would either shoot them or sell them into slavery. Lincoln signed an order promising revenge on Confederate prisoners of war if black soldiers were mistreated. Still, black prisoners were often dealt with more harshly than white prisoners. By the end of the Civil War, 16 black Union soldiers were awarded the Medal of Honor for their excellent service.

LIFE AFTER
the Civil War

HONORS FOR DOUGLASS

In 1874, Frederick Douglass was made president of the Freedman's Savings and Trust bank, which was set up to protect the money of former slaves and black Union soldiers. However, the bank didn't last long. He was then made a US marshal in 1877, the first African American appointed to a position approved by the US Senate. Douglass was also the US ambassador to Haiti, a post he held from 1889 to 1891.

After the Civil War ended in 1865, a period called Reconstruction began. During this time, the former Confederate states established new state governments in order to be accepted back into the Union.

However, **discrimination** didn't end there. Acts called "Jim Crow laws" were put in place to keep blacks from exercising their new rights. Frederick Douglass worried that not enough was being done: *"You say you have emancipated us. You have; and I thank you for it. But what is your emancipation? . . . You turned us loose to the sky, to the storm, to the whirlwind, and, worst of all, you turned us loose to the wrath of our infuriated masters."* Many Jim Crow laws would remain in place until the 1960s.

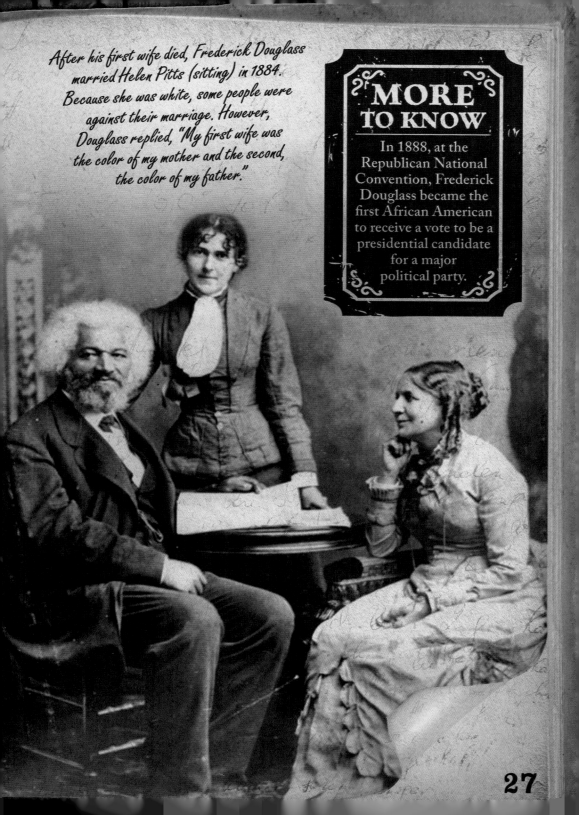

After his first wife died, Frederick Douglass married Helen Pitts (sitting) in 1884. Because she was white, some people were against their marriage. However, Douglass replied, "My first wife was the color of my mother and the second, the color of my father."

MORE TO KNOW

In 1888, at the Republican National Convention, Frederick Douglass became the first African American to receive a vote to be a presidential candidate for a major political party.

The PASSING
of an American Legend

Frederick Douglass was tireless in his fight to win freedom for all Americans, and he continued to serve his country as well as fight for the rights of those who had few. On February 20, 1895, Frederick Douglass attended a meeting of the National Council of Women in Washington, DC, where the audience clapped for him. Later that day, he died at his home.

MORE TO KNOW

The first-ever monument to a black American was created in honor of Frederick Douglass in Rochester, New York, in 1898.

At his funeral, thousands of people lined up to view the coffin and show their respect and admiration. Newspapers across the world remembered the great man who, according to his *New York Times* **obituary**, *"won for himself the esteem and reverence of all fair-minded persons, both in this country and in Europe."* Today, he's remembered as someone who worked for the betterment of all people.

TIMELINE
THE LIFE OF FREDERICK DOUGLASS

Frederick Augustus Washington Bailey is born a slave — **1817 OR 1818**

1826 — Sent to Baltimore, Maryland

Tries but fails to escape — **1833**

1836 — Again tries but fails to escape

Escapes to the North — **1838**

1841 — Attends antislavery convention and is asked to speak

Publishes the first of three autobiographies — **1845**

1846 — Is made a free man, thanks to two women who buy his freedom

Attends Seneca Falls convention for women's suffrage — **1848**

1861 — Civil War begins; works for equal pay for black soldiers

Is nominated as the US vice president for the Equal Rights Party — **1872**

1874 — Is made president of Freedman's Savings and Trust

Is appointed US marshal — **1877**

1888 — Receives a vote for becoming a presidential candidate for the Republican Party

Is made US ambassador to Haiti — **1889**

1895 — Dies on February 20

MEMORIES OF A GREAT MAN

Much of what we know about Douglass's life and works is because of Helen Pitts. Helen borrowed money to buy Douglass's Cedar Hill home in Washington, DC, from the Douglass children to found the Frederick Douglass Memorial and Historical Association. Later, the National Association of Colored Women bought the home and, with the help of the government, turned it into a National Historic Site.

GLOSSARY

authentic: shown to be true and trustworthy

autobiography: a book written by someone about their life

caulker: one who makes a boat watertight by filling in cracks with waterproof material

convention: a gathering of people who have a common interest or purpose

deference: polite respect

discrimination: unfairly treating people unequally because of their race or beliefs

emancipation: the act of freeing from the restraint, control, or power of another, usually referring to the freeing of slaves

immigrant: one who comes to a new country to settle there

infuriated: extremely angry

obituary: an announcement, especially in a newspaper, of somebody's death

oppression: the unjust use of power over another

Quaker: one who belongs to a faith that believes in equality for all people, strong families and communities, and peace

reluctant: feeling unwilling

suffragist: one who fights for suffrage, or the right to vote

FOR MORE
Information

Books

Ruffin, Frances E. *Frederick Douglass: A Powerful Voice for Freedom*. New York, NY: Sterling Publishing, 2008.

Vander Hook, Sue. *Frederick Douglass: Fugitive Slave and Abolitionist*. Edina, MN: ABDO, 2011.

Weiss, Lynne. *Frederick Douglass and the Abolitionist Movement*. New York, NY: PowerKids Press, 2014.

Websites

Frederick Douglass Honor Society
www.frederickdouglasshonorsociety.org
Find out more about Douglass's life on this site.

Frederick Douglass National Historic Site
www.nps.gov/frdo/index.htm
Read about the home of Frederick Douglass, and plan a trip to visit.

The Life and Times of Frederick Douglass
docsouth.unc.edu/neh/dougl92/menu.html
Read Douglass's autobiography for free online.

INDEX

abolition 8, 14, 18, 20, 21
Auld, Hugh 6, 8
Auld, Sophia 6, 7
autobiographies 4, 5, 11,
        29
Bailey, Frederick
        Augustus
        Washington 4, 29
Baltimore, Maryland 6,
        8, 10, 29
blacks in Union army 23,
        24, 25, 29
children 13, 25, 29
citizenship for blacks 24,
        25
Civil War 22, 23, 24, 25,
        26, 29
Douglass in politics 20,
        26, 27, 29
Emancipation
        Proclamation 22
escape 6, 8, 9, 10, 11, 12,
        15, 29
Europe 16, 18, 28
freedom purchased 19, 29

Garrison, William Lloyd
        14, 15, 17
Jim Crow laws 26
learning to read 6, 7
learning to write 6, 8
Lincoln, Abraham 22,
        23, 25
Massachusetts
        Anti-Slavery Society
        15
Murray, Anna 8, 10, 12,
        13, 27
Narrative of the Life of
        Frederick Douglass,
        an American Slave
        5, 16, 17
New York City 8, 12
North 5, 9, 10, 12, 13, 20,
        22, 23, 29
North Star 20
Pitts, Helen 27, 29
South 5, 6, 22, 23
Underground Railroad 9
women's suffrage 20, 21,
        29